Daily Spanish FOR DUMMIES®

POCKET EDITION

by Susana Wald

BICENTENNIAL 1807 WILEY 2007 BICENTENNIAL

Wiley Publishing, Inc.

Daily Spanish For Dummies®, Pocket Edition

Published by
Wiley Publishing, Inc.
111 River St.
Hoboken, NJ 07030-5774
www.wiley.com

For general information on our other products and services, please contact our Customer Care Department within the U.S. at 800-762-2974, outside the U.S. at 317-572-3993, or fax 317-572-4002.

For technical support, please visit www.wiley.com/techsupport.

Wiley also publishes its books in a variety of electronic formats. Some content that appears in print may not be available in electronic books.

ISBN: 978-0-470-05568-7

Manufactured in the United States of America

10 9 8 7 6 5 4 3 2

1S/QZ/QR/QX/IN

Daily Spanish FOR DUMMIES®

POCKET EDITION

Table of Contents

Introduction *1*
About This Book 1
Conventions Used in This Book 2
Icons Used in This Book 3
Where to Go from Here 3

Chapter 1: You Already Know a Little Spanish *5*
You Already Know Some Spanish 6
Beware of false friends 6
Recognize some crossover influence 7
Reciting Your ABCs 8
Consonants 10
Vowels 18
The diphthongs 21
Pronunciation and Stress 23
Looking for stress, normally 23
Looking for accented vowels 24
Understanding accents on diphthongs 24
¡Punctuation Plus 25
Some Basic Phrases to Know 25

Chapter 2: Talking the Talk: Having a Conversation *27*
¡Buenos Dias! Hello! Greetings and Introductions 27
Using names and surnames 28
Introductions: Solemn and social 31
Getting to Know You: Making Small Talk 32
Using the key questions: Seven Ws and an H 33
People and families 34

Talking on the Phone 35
Opening lines 35
Dealing with "porridge": When you can't make out the words 36

Chapter 3: Dining Out and Going to Market......................................39

¡Buen Provecho Enjoy Your Meal 39
Table terms 40
Phrases for food and drink 40
Three Verbs Used at the Table 42
To take and to drink: The verb tomar 42
For drinking only: The verb beber 43
For eating: The verb comer 44
At the Restaurant: Trying Exotic Foods 44
At the Market 48
Buying fruit 49
Buying vegetables 50
Shopping for fish 51
At the Supermercado 52

Introduction

As society becomes more international in nature, knowing how to say at least a few words in other languages becomes increasingly useful. Inexpensive airfares make travel abroad a more realistic option. Global business environments necessitate overseas travel. You just may have friends and neighbors who speak other languages, or you may want to get in touch with your heritage by learning a little bit of the language that your ancestors spoke.

Whatever your reason for wanting to acquire some Spanish, *Daily Spanish For Dummies* can help. This book gives you the skills you need for basic communication in Spanish. We're not promising fluency here, but if you want to greet someone, make small talk, or order off a menu in Spanish, you need look no further than *Daily Spanish For Dummies.*

About This Book

Use the text as a language and cultural guide for those moments when you really need to know how and why things are done. This book concentrates on Latin American Spanish, meaning the Spanish spoken in Central and South American countries.

You can use *Daily Spanish For Dummies* however you want to, whether your goal is to know some words and phrases to help you get around when you visit the countries of Central or South America, travel to Spain, or simply want to be able to say, "Hello, how are you?" to your Spanish-speaking neighbor.

Conventions Used in This Book

To make this book easy for you to navigate, we've set up a couple of conventions:

- Spanish terms are set in **boldface** to make them stand out.
- Pronunciations, set in *italics,* follow the Spanish terms.
- Verb conjugations (lists that show you the forms of a verb) are given in tables in this order: the *I* form, the *you* (singular) form, the *he/she/it* form, the *we* form, the *you* (plural/formal) form, and the *they* form. Pronunciations follow in the second column.

Also note that because each language has its own ways of expressing ideas, the English translations that we provide for the Spanish terms may not be exactly literal. We want you to know the gist of what's being said, not just the words that are being said. For example, you can translate the Spanish phrase **de nada** *(deh nah-dah)* literally as "of nothing," but the phrase really means "you're welcome." This book gives the "you're welcome" translation.

Icons Used in This Book

You may be looking for particular information while reading this book. To make certain types of information easier for you to find, we've placed the following icons in the left-hand margins throughout the book:

This icon highlights tips that can make learning Spanish easier.

Languages are full of quirks that may trip you up if you're not prepared for them. This icon points to discussions of these weird grammar rules.

If you're looking for information and advice about culture and travel, look for these icons. They draw your attention to interesting tidbits about the countries in which Spanish is spoken.

Where to Go from Here

You've got your copy of *Daily Spanish For Dummies* — now what? Learning a language is all about jumping in and giving it a try (no matter how bad your pronunciation is at first). So make the leap! Consider the basics of Spanish with Chapter 1, head straight to Chapter 2 for all things conversational, and turn to Chapter 3 for food-related terms. If you want even more information on Spanish, from using idioms and popular expressions to getting around in a Spanish-speaking country, check out *Spanish For Dummies,* the book on which this one was based — simply head to your local book seller or go to www.dummies.com!

Chapter 1

You Already Know a Little Spanish

In This Chapter

- Recognizing the little Spanish you know
- Saying it right: Basic pronunciation
- Using gestures
- Understanding typical expressions

If you're familiar with the term *Latin lover,* you may not be surprised to know that Spanish is called a Romance language. But the romance we're talking about here isn't exactly the Latin-lover type — unless you love to learn Latin.

Spanish is a Romance language because it has its origins in the Latin of ancient Rome. Because of that common origin, Romance languages have many similarities in grammar and the way they sound. (The fact that they all sound so romantic when spoken is purely a bonus!) For example, **casa** *(kah-sah),* the word for *house,* is identical in looks, meaning, and sound whether you speak Portuguese, Italian, or Spanish.

You Already Know Some Spanish

The English language is like an ever-growing entity that, with great wisdom, absorbs what it needs from other cultures and languages. English is also a language that is like a bouquet of flowers plucked from many different roots. One of these roots is Latin, which 2,000 years ago was spread all over Europe by the Romans and later by scholars of the Middle Ages.

Because all of these live elements exist in the root of the language, you can find many correspondences between English and Spanish in the words that come from both Latin and French roots. These words can cause both delight and embarrassment. The delight comes in the words where the coincident sounds also give similar meanings. The embarrassment comes from words where the sounds and even the roots are the same, but the meanings are completely different.

Among the delightful discoveries of similarities between the languages are words like **soprano** *(soh-prah-noh)* (soprano), **pronto** *(prohn-toh)* (right away; soon), and thousands of others that differ by just one or two letters such as **conclusión** *(kohn-kloo-seeohn)* (conclusion), **composición** *(kohm-poh-see-see- ohn)* (composition), **libertad** (lee-bvehr-tahd) (liberty), **economía** *(eh-koh-noh-meeah)* (economy), **invención** *(een-bvehn-seeohn)* (invention), and **presidente** *(preh-see-dehn-teh)* (president).

Beware of false friends

The trouble begins in the world of words that French linguists have designated as "false friends." You can't trust fool's gold, false friends, or all word similarities. Within the groups of false friends, you may find words that look very similar and even have the same root, yet mean completely different things. One that comes to mind is the word *actual,* which has very different meanings in English and Spanish. In English, you know that it means "real; in reality; or the very one." Not so in Spanish. **Actual** *(ahk-tooahl)* in Spanish means "present; current; belonging to this moment, this day, or this year."

So, for example, when you say "the actual painting" in English, you're referring to the real one, the very one people are looking at or want to see. But, when you say **la pintura actual** *(lah peen-too-rah ahk-tooahl)* in Spanish, you're referring to the painting that belongs to the current time, the one that follows present-day trends — a modern painting.

Another example is the adjective *embarrassed,* that in English means "ashamed" or "encumbered." In Spanish, **embarazada** *(ehm-bvah-rah-sah-dah)* is the adjective that comes from the same root as the English word, yet its use nowadays almost exclusively means "pregnant." So you can say in English that you are a little embarrassed, but in Spanish you can't be just a little **embarazada.** Either you're pregnant or you're not.

Recognize some crossover influence

Word trouble ends at the point where a word originating in English is absorbed into Spanish or vice versa. The proximity of the United States to Mexico produces a change in the Spanish spoken there. An example is the word *car.* In Mexico, people say **carro** *(kah-rroh).* In South America, on the other hand, people say **auto** *(ahoo-toh).* In Spain, people say **coche** *(koh-cheh).*

Here are just a few examples of Spanish words that you already know because English uses them, too:

- You've been to a **rodeo** *(roh-deh-oh)* or a **fiesta** *(feeehs-tah).*
- You've probably taken a **siesta** *(seeehs-tah)* or two.
- You probably know at least one **señorita** *(seh-nyoh-ree-tah),* and you surely have an **amigo** *(ah-mee-goh).* Maybe you'll even see him **mañana** *(mah-nyah-nah).*
- You already know the names of places like **Los Angeles** *(lohs ahn-Heh-lehs)* (the angels), **San Francisco** *(sahn frahn-sees-koh)* (St. Francis), **La Jolla** *(la Hoh-yah)* (the jewel), **Florida** *(floh-ree-dah)* (the blooming one), and **Puerto Rico** *(pooehr-toh ree-koh)* (rich harbor).
- You've eaten a **tortilla** *(tohr-tee-lyah),* a **taco** *(tah-koh),* or a **burrito** *(bvoo-rree-toh).*
- You fancy the **tango** *(tahn-goh),* the **bolero** *(bvo-leh-roh),* or the **rumba** *(room-bvah),* or you may dance the **cumbia** *(koom-bveeah).*
- You have a friend named **Juanita** *(Hooah-nee-tah),* **Anita** *(ah-nee-tah),* or **Clara** *(klah-rah).*

Reciting Your ABCs

Correct pronunciation is key to avoiding misunderstandings. The following sections present some basic guidelines for proper pronunciation.

Next to the Spanish words throughout this book, the pronunciation is in parentheses, which we call *pronunciation brackets.* Within the pronunciation brackets, we separate all the words that have more than one syllable with a hyphen, like this: *(kah-sah).* An underlined syllable within the pronunciation brackets tells you to accent, or stress, that syllable. We say much more about stress later in this chapter. In the meantime, don't let yourself get stressed out (pardon the pun). We explain each part of the language separately, and the pieces will quickly fall into place. Promise!

In the following section, we comment on some letters of the alphabet from the Spanish point of view. The aim is to help you to understand Spanish pronunciations. Here is the basic Spanish alphabet and its pronunciation:

- **a** *(ah)*
- **b** *(bveh)*
- **c** *(seh)*
- **d** *(deh)*
- **e** *(eh)*
- **f** *(eh-feh)*
- **g** *(Heh)*
- **h** *(ah-cheh)*
- **i** *(ee)*
- **j** *(Hoh-tah)*
- **k** *(kah)*
- **l** *(eh-leh)*
- **m** *(eh-meh)*
- **n** *(eh-neh)*

- **ñ** *(eh-nyeh)*
- **o** *(oh)*
- **p** *(peh)*
- **q** *(koo)*
- **r** *(eh-reh)*
- **s** *(eh-seh)*
- **t** *(teh)*
- **u** *(oo)*
- **v** *(bveh)*
- **w** *(doh-bleh bveh) (oobveh doh-bvleh)* (Spain)
- **x** *(eh-kees)*
- **y** *(ee gree eh-gah)*
- **z** *(seh-tah)*

Spanish also includes some double letters in its alphabet: **ch** *(cheh),* **ll** *(ye),* and **rr** *(a trilled r).*

We don't go through every letter of the alphabet in the sections that follow, only those that you use differently in Spanish than in English. The differences can lie in pronunciation, the way they look, in the fact that you seldom see the letters, or that you don't pronounce them at all.

Consonants

Consonants tend to sound the same in English and Spanish. We explain the few differences that you can find.

Inside the Spanish-speaking world itself, you'll find that consonants may be pronounced differently than in English. For example, in Spain the consonant **z** is pronounced like the **th** in the English word *thesis.* (Latin Americans don't use this sound; in all 19 Spanish-speaking countries on this hemisphere, **z** and **s** sound the same.)

In the Spanish speaker's mind, a consonant is any sound that needs to have a vowel next to it when you pronounce it. For example, saying the letter **t** by itself may be difficult for a Spanish speaker. To the Spanish ear, pronouncing **t** sounds like **te** *(teh).* Likewise, the Spanish speaker says **ese** *(eh-seh)* when pronouncing the letter **s.**

Only a few consonants in Spanish differ from their English counterparts. The following sections look more closely at the behavior and pronunciation of these consonants.

The letter K

In Spanish, the letter **k** is used only in words that have their origin in foreign languages. More often than not, this letter is seen in **kilo** *(kee-loh),* meaning *thousand* in Greek. An example is **kilómetro** *(kee-loh-meh-troh)* (kilometer) — a thousand-meter measure for distance.

The letter H

In Spanish, the letter **h** is *always* mute. That's it!

The pronunciation brackets throughout this book often include the letter **h.** These h's generally signal certain vowel sounds, which we cover later in this chapter.

In the pronunciation brackets, the Spanish **h** simply doesn't appear, because it's mute.

Following are some examples of the Spanish "h":

- **Huayapan** *(ooah-yah-pahn)* (name of a village in Mexico)
- **hueso** *(ooeh-soh)* (bone)
- **huevo** *(ooeh-bvoh)* (egg)

The letter J

The consonant **j** sounds like a guttural **h.** Normally you say **h** quite softly, as though you were just breathing out. Now, say your **h,** but gently raise the back of your tongue, as if you were saying **k.** Push the air out real hard, and you'll get the sound. Try it! There — it sounds like you're gargling, doesn't it?

To signal that you need to make this sound, we use a capital letter *H* within the pronunciation brackets.

Now try the sound out on these words:

- **Cajamarca** *(kah-Hah-mahr-kah)* (the name of a city in Peru)
- **cajeta** *(kah-Heh-tah)* (a delicious, thick sauce made of milk and sugar)
- **cajón** *(kah-Hohn)* (big box)
- **jadeo** *(Hah-deh-oh)* (panting)
- **Jijón** *(Hee-Hohn)* (the name of a city in Spain)
- **jota** *(Hoh-tah)* (the Spanish name for the letter **j;** also the name of a folk dance in Spain.)
- **tijera** *(tee-Heh-rah)* (scissors)

The letter C

The letter **c,** in front of the vowels **a, o,** and **u,** sounds like the English **k.** We use the letter *k* in the pronunciation brackets to signal this sound. Following are some examples:

- **acabar** *(ah-kah-bvahr)* (to finish)
- **café** *(kah-feh)* (coffee)
- **casa** *(kah-sah)* (house)
- **ocaso** *(oh-kah-soh)* (sunset)

When the letter **c** is in front of the vowels **e** and **i,** it sounds like the English **s.** In the pronunciation brackets, we signal this sound as *s.* Following are some examples:

- **acero** *(ah-seh-roh)* (steel)
- **cero** *(seh-roh)* (zero)
- **cine** *(see-neh)* (cinema)

In much of Spain — primarily the north and central parts — the letter **c** is pronounced like the *th* in *thanks* when placed before the vowels **e** and **i.**

The letters S and Z

In Latin American Spanish, the letters **s** and **z** always sound like the English letter **s.** We use the letter *s* in the pronunciation brackets to signal this sound. Following are some examples:

- **asiento** *(ah-seeehn-toh)* (seat)
- **sol** *(sohl)* (sun)
- **zarzuela** *(sahr-sooeh-lah)* (Spanish-style operetta)

In Spain, **z** also has the sound of the *th* in *thanks,* rather than the **s** sound prevalent in Latin America.

The letters B and V

The letters **b** and **v** are pronounced the same, the sound being somewhere in-between the two letters. This in-between is a fuzzy, bland sound — closer to **v** than to **b.** If you position your lips and teeth to make a **v** sound, and then try to make a **b** sound, you'll have it. To remind you to make this sound, we use *bv* in our pronunciation brackets, for both **b** and **v.** Here are some examples:

- **cabeza** *(kah-bveh-sah)* (head)
- **vida** *(bvee-dah)* (life)
- **violín** *(bveeoh-leen)* (violin)

The letter Q

Spanish doesn't use the letter **k** very much; when the language wants a **k** sound in front of the vowels **e** and **i,** it unfolds the letter combination **qu.** So when you see the word **queso** *(keh-soh)* (cheese), you immediately know that you say the **k** sound. Here are some examples of the Spanish letter **q,** which we indicate by the letter *k* in pronunciation brackets:

- **Coquimbo** *(koh-keem-bvoh)* (the name of a city in Chile)
- **paquete** *(pah-keh-teh)* (package)
- **pequeño** *(peh-keh-nyoh)* (small)
- **tequila** *(teh-kee-lah)* (Mexican liquor, spirits)

The letter G

In Spanish the letter **g** has a double personality, like the letter **c.** When you combine the letter **g** with a consonant or when you see it in front of the vowels **a, o,** and **u,** it sounds like the **g** in *goose.* Here are some examples:

- **begonia** *(bveh-goh-neeah)* (begonia)
- **gato** *(gah-toh)* (cat)
- **gracias** *(grah-seeahs)* (thank you)
- **pagado** *(pah-gah-doh)* (paid for)

The **g** changes personality in front of the vowels **e** and **i.** It sounds like the Spanish **j,** which we signal with the capital *H* in our pronunciation brackets.

- **agenda** *(ah-Hehn-dah)* (agenda; date book)
- **gerente** *(Heh-rehn-teh)* (manager)

To hear the sound **g** (as in *goat*) in front of the vowels **e** and **i,** you must insert a **u,** making **gue** and **gui.** To remind you to make the goat sound (no, no, not *mme-hehe,* but **g**) we use *gh* in our pronunciation brackets. Some examples:

- **guía** *(gheeah)* (guide)
- **guiño** *(ghee-nyoh)* (wink)
- **guerra** *(gheh-rrah)* (war)

Double consonants

Spanish has two double consonants: ll and rr. They are considered a singular letter, and each has a singular sound. Because these consonants are considered singular, they stick together when you separate syllables.

For example, the word calle (kah-yeh) (street) appears as ca-lle. And torre (toh-rreh), (tower) separates into to-rre.

The letter LL

The **ll** consonant sounds like the **y** in the English word *yes,* except in Argentina and Uruguay.

Argentineans and Uruguayans pronounce this consonant as the sound that happens when you have your lips pursed to say **s** and then make the **z** sound through them. Try it. Fun, isn't it? But really, the sound isn't that difficult to make, because you can find the English equivalent in words like *measure* and *pleasure.* The way you say those **s** sounds is exactly how **ll** is pronounced in Argentina and Uruguay.

Throughout this book, we use the sound like the English **y** in the word *yes,* which is how **ll** is pronounced in 18 of the 20 Spanish-speaking countries. In the pronunciation brackets, we use *y* to signal this sound.

Now try the **ll** sound, using the **y** sound, in the following examples:

- **brillo** *(bvree-yoh)* (shine)
- **llama** *(yah-mah)* (flame; also the name of an animal in Peru)
- **lluvia** *(yoo-bveeah)* (rain)

The letter RR

The **rr** sounds like a strongly rolled **r.** In fact, every **r** is strongly rolled in Spanish, but the double one is the real winner. To roll an **r,** curl your tongue against the roof of your mouth as you finish the **r** sound. It should trill.

An easy way to make this sound is to say the letter **r** as though you were pretending to sound like an outboard motor. There. You have it! Spanish speakers take special pleasure in rolling their **rr**'s. One fun thing about **rr** is that no words begin with it. Isn't that a relief! In pronunciation brackets we simply signal this sound as **rr.**

Play with these words:

- **carrera** *(kah-rreh-rah)* (race; profession)
- **correo** *(koh-rreh-oh)* (mail, post)
- **tierra** *(teeeh-rrah)* (land)

The letter Y

This letter represents sounds that are very similar to those of **ll.** The people of both Argentina and Uruguay pronounce this sound differently from the rest of Latin America. We advise that you pronounce it as the English **y** in *yes* and *you.* In the pronunciation brackets, we signal this sound as *y.* Following are some examples:

- **playa** *(plah-yah)* (beach)
- **yema** *(yeh-mah)* (yolk; also finger tip)
- **yodo** *(yoh-doh)* (Iodine)

In Spanish, the letter **y** is never a vowel, always a consonant.

The letter Ñ

When you see a wiggly line on top of the letter **n** that looks like **ñ,** use the **ny** sound that you use for the English word *canyon.* The wiggly line is called a **tilde** *(teel-deh).* In pronunciation brackets, we show this sound as *ny.* Following are some examples:

- **cuñado** *(koo-nyah-doh)* (brother-in-law)
- **mañana** *(mah-nyah-nah)* (tomorrow)
- **niña** *(nee-nyah)* (girl)

Vowels

If you want your Spanish to sound like a native's, you have to concentrate on your *vowels.*

The biggest difference between English and Spanish is almost certainly in the way the vowels are written and pronounced. By now, you may be well aware that one vowel in English can have more than one sound. Look, for instance, at *fat* and *fate.* Both words have the vowel **a,** but they're pronounced much differently from each other. The good news is that in Spanish, you always say the vowels one way, and one way only.

The upcoming sections discuss the five vowels — which are the only vowel sounds in Spanish. They are **a** *(ah),* **e** *(eh),* **i** *(ee),* **o** *(oh),* **u** *(oo).* Spanish sees each of these vowels by itself and makes other sounds by combining the vowels in twos.

The vowel A

As children, almost everybody sings their ABCs. In Spanish, the English **a** that starts off the song, is pronounced *ah.* The easiest way to remember how to pronounce the letter **a** in Spanish is to sing the chorus of the Christmas carol "Deck the Halls" to yourself. You remember the chorus, don't you? *Fa la la la la, la la, la la.* We write this sound as *ah* in the pronunciation brackets.

Following are some sample words to practice. Remember that you pronounce each and every a exactly the same way.

- **Caracas** *(kah-rah-kas)* (a city in Venezuela)
- **mapa** *(mah-pah)* (map)
- **Guadalajara** *(gooah-dah-lah-Hah-rah)* (a city in Mexico)

The vowel E

To get an idea of how the Spanish **e** sounds, smile gently, open your mouth a bit and say "eh." The sound should be like the **e** in the English word *pen*. In our pronunciation brackets, this vowel appears as *eh*.

Try these:

- **pelele** *(peh-leh-leh)* (rag doll; puppet)
- **pelo** *(peh-loh)* (hair)
- **seco** *(seh-koh)* (dry)

The vowel I

In Spanish the vowel **i** sounds like the **ee** in *seen*, but just a touch shorter. To give you an example, when English speakers say *feet* or *street*, the Spanish speaker hears what sounds like almost two i's.

We signal this sound as *ee* in our pronunciation brackets. Following are some examples:

- **irritar** *(ee-rree-tahr)* (to irritate)
- **piña** *(pee-nyah)* (pineapple)
- **pintar** *(peen-tahr)* (to paint)

The vowel O

The Spanish put their mouths in a rounded position, as if to breathe a kiss over a flower, and keeping it in that position, say **o.** It sounds like the **o** in *floor,* but a bit shorter. We signal this sound as *oh* in the pronunciation brackets.

Try practicing the sound on these words:

- **coco** *(koh-koh)* (coconut)
- **Orinoco** *(oh-ree-noh-koh)* (a river in Venezuela)
- **Oruro** *(oh-roo-roh)* (a city in Bolivia)
- **toronja** *(toh-rohn-Hah)* (grapefruit)

The vowel U

The fifth and last vowel in Spanish is the **u,** and it sounds like the **oo** in *moon* or *raccoon,* but just a touch shorter. *Oo,* we think you've got it! We write this sound as *oo* in the pronunciation brackets. Here are some examples of the u sound:

- **cuna** *(koo-nah)* (cradle)
- **cuñado** *(koo-nyah-doh)* (brother-in-law)
- **cúrcuma** *(koor-koo-mah)* (turmeric)
- **curioso** *(koo-reeoh-soh)* (curious)
- **fruta** *(froo-tah)* (fruit)
- **luna** *(loo-nah)* (moon)
- **tuna** *(too-nah)* (prickly pear)

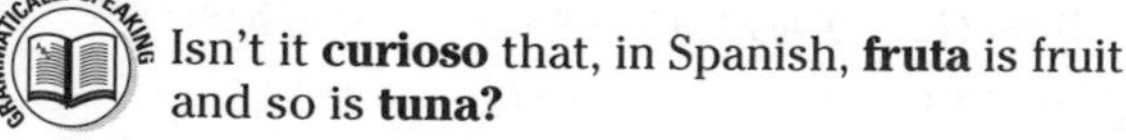

Isn't it **curioso** that, in Spanish, **fruta** is fruit and so is **tuna?**

The diphthongs

Good grief, you say, what's that?

Diphthong comes from Greek, where *di* means "two," and *thong* comes from a very similar word meaning "sound" or "voice." (Don't worry, we had to look it up in the dictionary ourselves.) Very simply, it means "double sound." There. That's easier.

The Spanish word is **diptongo** *(deep-tohn-goh)*. **Diptongos** are the combination of two vowels, from the Spanish-speaking point of view. For instance, **i** and **o** combine to make **io** as in **patio** *(pah-teeoh)* (courtyard or patio).

Joining the weak to the strong

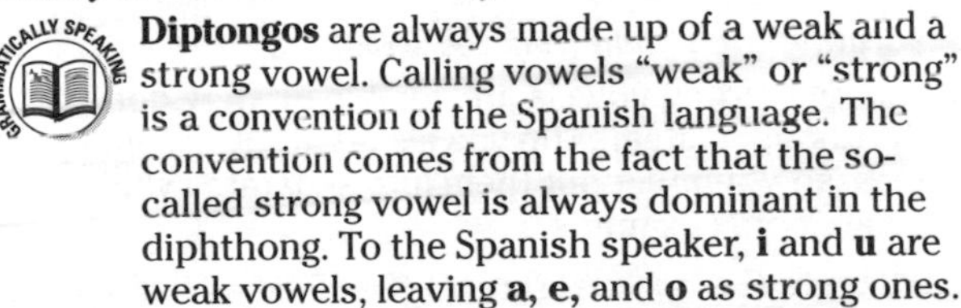

Diptongos are always made up of a weak and a strong vowel. Calling vowels "weak" or "strong" is a convention of the Spanish language. The convention comes from the fact that the so-called strong vowel is always dominant in the diphthong. To the Spanish speaker, **i** and **u** are weak vowels, leaving **a, e,** and **o** as strong ones.

To visualize this weak or strong concept, consider a piccolo flute and a bass horn. The sound of the piccolo is definitely more like the Spanish **i** and **u,** while the base horn sounds more like the Spanish **a, e,** and especially **o.**

Any combination of one strong and one weak vowel is a **diptongo** *(deep-tohn-goh),* which means that they will belong together in the same syllable. In fact, they're not only together, they're stuck like superglue; they can't be separated.

In the **diptongo,** the stress falls on the strong vowel (more about stress later in this chapter). An accent mark alerts you when the stress falls on the weak vowel. (More about accents later, too.) In the combination of two weak vowels, the stress is on the second one.

Try these examples of diphthongs:

- **bueno** *(bvooeh-noh)* (good)
- **cuando** *(kooahn-doh)* (when)
- **fiar** *(feeahr)* (sell on credit)
- **fuera** *(fooeh-rah)* (outside)
- **suizo** *(sooee-soh)* (Swiss)
- **viudo** *(bveeoo-doh)* (widower)

Separating the strong from the strong

When two strong vowels are combined, they don't form a diphthong. Instead, the vowels retain their separate values, so you must put them into separate syllables. Here are some examples:

- **aorta** *(ah-ohr-tah)* (aorta) (See! Just as in English!)
- **feo** *(feh-oh)* (ugly)
- **marea** *(mah-reh-ah)* (tide)
- **mareo** *(mah-reh-oh)* (dizziness)

Did you notice in the previous list how changing one letter, in **marea** and **mareo,** for example, can change the meaning of a word? This letter phenomenon occurs in Spanish, just as in English. Finding such words is fun.

In the case of the previous list, at least the two words come from the same root **mar** *(mahr)* (sea). And, associating the tide to one's dizziness isn't all that difficult. But in other places you can have oceans of difference. Here are some more examples: **casa** *(kah-sah)* (house) and **cosa** *(koh-sah)* (thing); and **pito** *(pee-toh)* (whistle), **pato** *(pah-toh)* (duck), and **peto** *(peh-toh)* (bib or breastplate.)

Pronunciation and Stress

In Spanish, one syllable is stressed in every word. *Stress* is the accent that you put on a syllable as you speak it. One syllable always gets more stress than the others. In single-syllable words, finding the stress is easy. But many words have more than one syllable, and that's when the situation becomes stressful.

Looking for stress, normally

Can you believe that you're *looking* for stress? In Spanish, the right stress at the right time is a good thing, and fortunately, stress in Spanish is easy to control. If you have *no* written accent, you have two possibilities:

- The word is stressed next to the last syllable if it ends in a vowel, an **n**, or an **s**. Here are some examples:
  - **camas** *(kah-mahs)* (beds)
  - **mariposas** *(mah-ree-poh-sahs)* (butterflies)
  - **pollo** *(poh-yoh)* (chicken)

- The word is stressed on the last syllable when it ends in a consonant that is not an **n** or **s.** Look at these examples:
  - **cantar** *(kahn-tahr)* (to sing)
  - **feliz** *(feh-lees)* (happy)

If a word is not stressed in either of these two ways, the word will have an accent mark on it to indicate where you should place the stress.

Looking for accented vowels

One good thing about having the accent mark on a vowel is that you can tell immediately where the stress is, just by looking at the word.

The accent mark does not affect how the vowel is pronounced, just which syllable is stressed.

Here are some examples of words with accent marks on a vowel:

- **balcón** *(bahl-kohn)* (balcony)
- **carácter** *(kah-rahk-tehr)* (character, personality)
- **fotógrafo** *(foh-toh-grah-foh)* (photographer)
- **pájaro** *(pah-Hah-roh)* (bird)

Understanding accents on diphthongs

An accent in a diphthong shows you which vowel to stress. Take a look at these examples:

- **¡Adiós!** *(ah-deeohs)* (Good-bye!)
- **¡Buenos días!** *(bvooeh-nohs deeahs)* (Good morning!)

- **¿Decía?** (deh-<u>see</u>ah) (You were saying?)
- **tía** (<u>tee</u>ah) (aunt)

¡Punctuation Plus

Did you notice the unfamiliar punctuation in **¡Buenos días!**, **¿Decía?**, and **¡Adiós!** (see the preceding section)? Spanish indicates the mood (or tone) of what you're saying both at the beginning and at the end of the phrase that is a question or an exclamation, as in **¿Decía?** *(deh-<u>see</u>ah)* (You were saying?) or **¡Decía!** *(deh<u>see</u>-ah)* (You were saying!).

As far as we know, Spanish is the only language that provides this sort of punctuation. However, this punctuation is very useful when you have to read something aloud because you know beforehand how to modulate your voice when the phrase is coming up.

This punctuation is the verbal equivalent of making gestures, which you can see in the following examples:

- **¿Dónde está?** *(<u>dohn</u>-deh ehs-<u>tah</u>)* (Where is it?)
- **¡Qué maravilla!** *(keh mah-rah-<u>bvee</u>-yah)* (How wonderful!)

Some Basic Phrases to Know

The following phrases can get you through a number of awkward pauses as you think of the right word:

- **¡Olé!** *(oh- <u>leh</u>)* (Great!; Superb!; Keep going!) This very Spanish expression is used during bullfights in Mexico and Peru.

- **¿Quiubo?** *(kee oo-boh)* (Hello, what's happening?)
- **¿De veras?** *(deh bveh-rahs)* (Really?) This phrase signals slight disbelief.
- **¡No me digas!** *(noh meh dee-gahs)* (You don't say!) This phrase also means disbelief.

Chapter 2

Talking the Talk: Having a Conversation

In This Chapter

- Meeting people and making introductions
- Chitchatting in Spanish
- Feeling comfortable on the phone

Your goal in learning Spanish likely has a lot to do with being able to communicate with people who speak it. In this chapter, we take you from greetings and introductions, through small talk, and to the phone.

¡Buenos Dias! Hello! Greetings and Introductions

In Latin America especially, *how* you greet people matters a great deal. Latin Americans tend to be very respectful of each other and of strangers. So as a rule, when you greet someone for the first time in Latin America, it's best not to say "Hello!" — a greeting that is quite informal.

Using names and surnames

Latin Americans are generally easygoing people who love to converse. If you feel interest on both your part and theirs to keep the contact going, then you can introduce yourself, but wait for your acquaintance to give you his or her name. Only if the other person doesn't give you his or her name should you ask what it is. In some specific situations, a third person introduces you, but usually you are expected to introduce yourself.

When you meet someone, he or she probably will tell you just his or her first name, or maybe only part of it — **Carmen** *(kahr-mehn),* instead of **María del Carmen** *(mah-reeah dehl kahr-mehn).* But, as you get to know people better, you'll learn their surnames, as well.

A new acquaintance usually expresses some caution in the beginning by giving you only a partial name. When you receive the full name and the two surnames, you know you have a complete introduction.

These little maneuvers take place because, in the Spanish-speaking world, it isn't customary to wait to be introduced to someone before you talk to him or her. An introduction as such isn't necessary. When a third party does introduce you, it's just meant to make your contact with the new acquaintance much faster.

What's in a name?

Suppose that you meet a woman named **María del Carmen Fernández Bustamante** *(mah-reeah dehl kahr-mehn fehr-nahn-dehs bvoos-tah-mahn-teh).* You can tell that you may call her **señorita** *(seh-nyoh-ree-tah),* or

Miss Fernández *(fehr-nahn-dehs)* because of the three-part structure of her name. (In an English-speaking country, she would rearrange her name to María del Carmen Bustamante Fernández because English speakers put the father's name at the end, and use the person's last name as a reference.)

So far, so good. But if Miss Fernández marries, she adds on more names. In our example, she marries **señor** *(seh-nyohr)* (Mr.) **Juan José García Díaz** *(Hooahn Hoh-seh gahr-seeah deeahs)*. She is still called Fernández, but after her father's name she adds **de** *(deh)* (of) and her husband's surname, which is García. Now, she is **señora María del Carmen Fernández de García** *(mah-reeah dehl kahr-mehn fehr-nahn-dehs deh gahr-seeah)*.

Only in abbreviations (as well as proper names) do Spanish speakers use capitals. Here's how it goes:

- **señor:** Sr.
- **señora:** Sra.
- **señorita:** Srta.
- **usted:** Ud.
- **ustedes:** Uds.

Within the social circles of some countries, the surname of a married woman's husband gets more emphasis; in other places, her father's surname is stressed. For example, you hear the husband's surname used more often in Argentina than in Mexico.

The effect of these conventions is that women keep their family names, which are considered very important and meaningful. A child's surnames indicate both his or her father and mother. Señor García, in our example, has a child, Mario, by a previous marriage to a woman whose surname was Ocampo. Because children carry the surnames of both parents, Mario is called Mario García Ocampo. And when señor García and María del Carmen Fernández de García's daughter, Ana, is born, her name is Ana García Fernández. Ana and Mario are siblings, having the same father and different mothers. The Spanish use of both the father's and mother's surnames immediately indicates the relationship between the siblings.

Among Spanish speaking peoples, using both parents' first names for their same-sex children is customary. So, in a family where the mother, Marta Inés, has three daughters, she may call one Marta Julieta, another Marta Felicia, and the third Marta Juana. When the father's name is used for the son, the two are called identical names, because "Jr." is not used in Spanish. But you can tell the men apart because their mother's surnames are different.

Introducing the verb llamarse

Now is a good time to include the conjugation of the **llamarse** *(yah-mahr-seh),* the equivalent of "name is," which you use when you introduce yourself.

The verb **llamar** is a regular **–ar** verb; however, the **se** at the end of it tells you that the verb is reflexive, which makes it irregular, too (nobody said grammar was easy). In case your memory needs to jog a little, a reflexive verb is one that acts on the noun (or object) of the sentence. For instance, the sentence **yo me llamo** *(yo meh yah-moh)* literally means "I call myself." In this case, "I" is the subject of the sentence and "call myself" reflects back to "I." Anytime you see the **se** at the end of a verb, you simply put the reflexive pronoun (**me** in the example sentence) in front of the verb.

Take a look at the Table 2-1 for the conjugation of **llamarse** in the present tense. Pay attention to the reflexive pronouns — they stay the same for all regular **–ar** verbs.

Table 2-1 The Conjugation of llamarse

Conjugation	*Pronunciation*
yo me llamo	yoh meh yah-moh
tú te llamas	too teh yah-mahs
él, ella, ello, uno, usted se llama	ehl, eh-yah, eh-yo, oo-noh, oos-tehd seh yah-mah
nosotros nos llamamos	noh-soh-trohs nohs yah-mah-mohs
vosotros os llamáis	bvoh-soh-trohs ohs yah-mahees
ellos, ellas, ustedes se llaman	eh-yohs, eh-yahs, oos-teh-dehs seh yah-mahn

Introductions: Solemn and social

Some situations call for a certain level of solemnity. An example is when you're being introduced to a very important or famous person.

Just as in English, a few, specific phrases signal this formality, as the following examples demonstrate:

- **¿Me permite presentarle a . . . .?** *(meh pehr-mee-teh preh-sehn-tahr-leh ah)* (May I introduce. . . .?)
- **Es un gusto conocerle.** *(ehs oon goos-toh koh-noh-sehr-leh)* (It's a pleasure to meet you.)
- **El gusto es mío.** *(ehl goos-toh ehs meeoh)* (The pleasure is mine.)

Introducing yourself formally

Introducing yourself formally means that you don't talk in a chummy, informal way to a person with whom you have no relationship as yet. You use the formal way of introducing yourself because you want to keep a certain distance, just in case you decide later on that you don't want a closer relationship with this person.

People who don't know each other use **usted** *(oos-tehd)* — the formal form of "you" — and its verbal form when addressing one another.

When you're talking to a child, you speak less formally. The adult speaker may be identified by the insertion of **don** in front of his name. Calling someone **don** (or the feminine form, **doña**) can be a way of showing that you're addressing an older and respected person. (To the child, the adult looks old.)

Getting to Know You: Making Small Talk

Meeting new people and getting to know them can be stressful, especially when you have to converse in a language that isn't your own. Small talk is the universally recognized means of joining a new situation by discussing common, easily understood interests and concerns. Through small talk, you can better understand how the people you come to know live and go about their lives. This section helps you make small talk with your Spanish-speaking neighbors so that you can begin to achieve a better understanding all around.

Using the key questions: Seven Ws and an H

You may have heard about "The Five W's," which represent the questions that you need to ask to cover the basic information about a situation (who, what, where, when, and why). We've added three more questions to this group that you may find useful when you meet someone. Here are the key questions:

- **¿Quién?** *(keeehn)* (Who?)
- **¿Qué?** *(keh)* (What?)
- **¿Dónde?** *(dohn-deh)* (Where?)
- **¿Cuándo?** *(kooahn-doh)* (When?)
- **¿Por qué?** *(pohr keh)* (Why?)
- **¿Cómo?** *(koh-moh)* (How?)
- **¿Cuánto?** *(kooahn-toh)* (How much?)
- **¿Cuál?** *(kooahl)* (Which?)

The following are examples of how to use these words:

- **¿Quién es él?** *(keeehn ehs ehl)* (Who is he?)
- **¿Qué hace usted?** *(keh ah-seh oos-tehd)* (What do you do?)

- **¿Dónde viven?** *(dohn-deh bvee-bvehn)* (Where do you live?)
- **¿Cuándo llegaron?** *(kooahn-doh yeh-gah-rohn)* (When did you arrive?)
- **¿Por qué está aquí?** *(pohr keh ehs-tah ah-kee)* (Why are you [formal] here? Why is he [she, it] here?)
- **¿Cómo es el camino?** *(koh-moh ehs ehl kah-mee-noh)* (What's the road like?)
- **¿Cuánto cuesta el cuarto?** *(kooahn-toh kooehs-tah ehl kooahr-toh)* (How much is the room?)
- **¿Cuál hotel es mejor?** *(kooahl oh-tehl ehs meh-Hohr)* (Which hotel is better?)

People and families

The individual is the basic element of U.S. and Canadian societies. In Latin America, on the other hand, the family is the basic unit. People work, live, and function in consonance with their families. When visiting your Spanish-speaking neighbors, therefore, you'll be more comfortable if you pay attention to the way that Latinos stress the importance of the family and of family relationships.

The following list gives basic names for family members:

- **padre** *(pah-dreh)* (father)
- **madre** *(mah-dreh)* (mother)
- **hijo** *(ee-Hoh)* (son)
- **hija** *(ee-Hah)* (daughter)
- **hermano** *(ehr-mah-noh)* (brother)

- **hermana** *(ehr-mah-nah)* (sister)
- **yerno** *(yehr-noh)* (son-in-law)
- **nuera** *(nooeh-rah)* (daughter-in-law)
- **nieto** *(neeeh-toh)* (grandson)
- **nieta** *(neeeh-tah)* (granddaughter)
- **cuñado** *(koo-nyah-doh)* (brother-in-law)
- **cuñada** *(koo-nyah-dah)* (sister-in-law)
- **primo** *(pree-moh)* (cousin [male])
- **prima** *(pree-mah)* (cousin [female])
- **padrino** *(pah-dree-noh)* (godfather)
- **madrina** *(mah-dree-nah)* (godmother)
- **tío** *(teeoh)* (uncle)
- **tía** *(teeah)* (aunt)
- **abuelo** *(ah-bvooeh-loh)* (grandfather)
- **abuela** *(ah-bvooeh-lah)* (grandmother)

Talking on the Phone

When you're first learning a language, being able to see the person you're talking to can be a big help in understanding what they mean. If you're intimidated by the thought of conducting a conversation in Spanish over the phone, read on.

Opening lines

So you punch in or dial a phone number — then what?

- Argentinians say **¡Holá!** *(ohlah)*.
- Chileans say **¡Aló!** *(ah-loh)*.

- Mexicans say **¡Bueno!** *(bvooeh-noh).*
- Spaniards say **¡Sí!**

These words all mean "Hello!" Most Spanish-speaking countries use **aló,** in the Chilean way.

These phrases come in very handy when you use the phone:

- **llamar por teléfono** *(yah-mahr pohr teh-leh-foh-noh)* (make a phone call)
- **marcar el número** *(mahr-kahr ehl noo-meh-roh)* (dial/punch in the number)
- **colgar** *(kohl-gahr)* (hang up)
- **la línea está libre** *(lah lee-neah ehs-tah lee-bvreh)* (the line is open)
- **la línea está ocupada** *(lah lee-neh-ah ehs-tah oh-koo-pah-dah)* (the line is busy)
- **el teléfono no responde** *(ehl teh-leh-foh-noh noh rehs-pohn-deh)* (there's no answer)

Dealing with "porridge": When you can't make out the words

When learning a language, you may find that some people you talk to speak too fast for you. You can't make out the words; everything seems mushy, like porridge. On the phone, fast talking is even more of a problem. You don't see the person, so you can't get the gist of the communication from body language or facial expressions.

Don't be too hard on yourself. Gently insist that the other person repeat the sentence more clearly. You're not being rude in the least; you simply didn't get the whole message, so you're asking for a repeat. No harm there.

The person you're talking to may have similar difficulties, even if the language is his own, so please be just as patient with him as you'd like him to be with you.

Chapter 3

Dining Out and Going to Market

In This Chapter

- Getting food and drink
- Asking simple questions at the restaurant
- Knowing food and utensil vocabulary

Food is an important element of any culture. Each country and region in Latin America has different-tasting food, making restaurant hopping and trying new dishes there among the most diverse experiences possible. The same is true in sunny Spain, where deep-fried fish, mountain-cured ham, and a variety of other tasty treats await you.

¡Buen Provecho Enjoy Your Meal

As with any cultural group, some peoples of Latin America are more interested in food than others. Mexicans are as devoted to their food as the French or the Chinese, even in very small places. They have very fine palates and can distinguish among many different fiery flavors. They also have an immense variety of ways to prepare the same foods, such as tortillas and beans, which are basic elements in their meals.

Table terms

You may find these phrases useful when you plan a meal:

- **¡A poner la mesa!** *(ah poh-nehr lah meh-sah)* (Set the table!)
- **Aquí están los platos y los vasos.** *(ah-kee ehs-tahn lohs plah-tohs ee lohs bvah-sohs)* (Here are the dishes and glasses.)
- **¿Qué cubiertos?** *(keh koo-bvee-ehr-tohs)* (What cutlery?)
- **Cuchara, cuchillo, tenedor, y cucharita.** *(koo-chah-rah koo-chee-yo teh-neh-dohr ee koo-chah-ree-tah)* (Spoon, knife, fork, and coffee or demitasse spoon.)
- **Aquí están las servilletas.** *(ah-kee ehs-tahn lahs sehr-bvee-yeh-tahs)* (Here are the napkins.)
- **Más sal en el salero.** *(mahs sahl ehn ehl sah-leh-roh)* (More salt in the salt shaker.)

Phrases for food and drink

Here are some common terms connected with meals:

- **almuerzo** *(ahl-mooehr-soh)* (lunch)
- **cena** *(seh-nah)* (supper)
- **comida** *(koh-mee-dah)* (dinner)
- **desayuno** *(deh-sah-yoo-noh)* (breakfast)

- **tengo sed** *(tehn-goh sehd)* (I'm thirsty)
- **tiene hambre** *(tee eh-neh ahm-bvreh)* (he/she's hungry)

You may hear these phrases, or speak them yourself, when giving or receiving foods and beverages:

- **¡Buen provecho!** *(bvooehn proh-bveh-choh)* (Enjoy your meal! — the equivalent of the French *Bon appetit!*)
- **¿Con qué está servido?** *(kohn keh ehs-tah sehr-bvee-doh)* (What does it come with?)
- **Está caliente.** *(ehs-tah kah-lee ehn-teh)* (It's hot [temperature].)
- **Está frío.** *(ehs-tah freeoh)* (It's cold.)
- **Está picante.** *(ehs-tah pee-kahn-teh)* (It's hot (flavor/spicy.)
- **Es sabroso.** *(ehs sah-bvroh-soh)* (It's tasty.)
- **Lamento, no tenemos . . .** *(lah-mehn-toh noh teh-neh-mohs)* (Sorry, we don't have any . . .)
- **¿Qué ingredientes tiene?** *(keh een-greh-dee ehn-tehs tee eh-neh)* (What are the ingredients?)
- **¿Qué más trae el plato?** *(keh mahs trah-eh ehl plah-toh)* (What else is in the dish?)

These words can help you when you're ordering something to drink:

- **Escoger un vino.** *(ehs-koh-Hehr oon bvee-noh)* (Choose a wine)
- **¡Salud!** *(sah-lood)* (Cheers!)
- **Tomar un refresco.** *(toh-mahr oon reh-frehs-koh)* (Drink a soda pop)

- **Tomar un trago.** *(toh-mahr oon trah-goh)* (Have a drink [alcoholic])
- **Un vaso de agua.** *(oon bvah-soh deh ah-gooah)* (A glass of water)
- **Un vaso de leche.** *(oon bvah-soh deh leh-cheh)* (A glass of milk)

Three Verbs Used at the Table

Insofar as talking about drinking goes, in Spanish, you do it with two verbs. One is **tomar** *(toh-mahr);* the other is **beber** *(bveh-bvehr).*

To take and to drink: The verb tomar

Tomar *(toh-mahr)* means literally "to take" and often means exactly that. But when you say **tomar un refresco** *(toh-mahr oon reh-frehs-koh),* you're talking about drinking a soda, not literally taking one, and you know that's what you mean because **tomar** is followed by something you drink. So **tomar** is a verb with a certain imprecision.

Tomar is a regular verb of the **–ar** *(ahr)* group. The root of the verb is **tom–** *(tohm),* as you can see from Table 3-1.

Table 3-1 The Conjugation of tomar

Conjugation	*Pronunciation*
yo tomo	yoh toh-moh
tú tomas	too toh-mahs

Conjugation	Pronunciation
él, ella, ello, uno, usted toma	ehl, eh-yah, eh-yoh, oo-noh, oos-tehd toh-mah
nosotros tomamos	noh-soh-trohs toh-mah-mohs
vosotros tomáis	bvoh-soh-trohs toh-mah-ees
ellos, ellas, ustedes toman	eh-yohs, eh-yahs, oos-teh-dehs toh-mahn

For drinking only: The verb beber

In the case of the verb **beber,** you can have no doubts: This verb applies to drinking only.

Beber *(bveh-bvehr)* is also a regular verb; it's from the **–er** *(ehr)* group. The root of the verb is: **beb–** *(bvehbv),* as you can see in Table 3-2.

Table 3-2 The Conjugation of beber

Conjugation	Pronunciation
yo bebo	yoh bveh-bvoh
tú bebes	too bveh-bvehs
él, ella, ello, uno, usted bebe	ehl, eh-yah, eh-yoh, oo-noh oos-tehd bveh-bveh
nosotros bebemos	noh-soh-trohs bveh-bveh-mohs
vosotros bebéis	bvoh-soh-trohs bveh-bvehees
ellos, ellas, ustedes beben	eh-yohs, eh-yahs, oos-teh-dehs bveh-bvehn

For eating: The verb comer

Comer *(kohm-ehr)* means "to eat." A regular verb from the **–er** *(ehr)* group, the root of this verb is **com** *(kohm)*, as Table 3-3 shows.

Table 3-3 The Conjugation of comer

Conjugation	Pronunciation
yo como	yoh koh-moh
tú comes	too koh-mehs
él, ella, ello, uno, usted come	ehl, eh-yah, eh-yoh, oo-noh, oos-tehd koh-meh
nosotros comemos	noh-soh-trohs koh-meh-mohs
vosotros coméis	bvoh-soh-trohs koh-mehees
ellos, ellas, ustedes comen	eh-yohs, eh-yahs, oos-teh-dehs koh-mehn

At the Restaurant: Trying Exotic Foods

A menu in a foreign language can be intimidating. But Latin America has many tasty and exotic foods that you won't want to miss. This list identifies the most popular ones:

- **Agua** *(ah-gooah)* in Mexico can mean "water," which is its exact translation, but it can also be a beverage made with water, fruit, and sugar. All fruits, and some vegetables even, make refreshing **aguas** *(ah-gooahs)*.

- **Aguita** *(ah-goo-ee-tah)* little water, in Chile can be an herb tea, served after a meal.
- **Empanada** *(ehm-pah-nah-dah)* actually means "in bread." In Mexico, an **empanada** is a folded and stuffed corn **tortilla.** You can get **empanadas** made out of wheat dough, which is then folded and stuffed, in Argentina and Chile. Argentineans like theirs small. Chileans make theirs big. Either way, they're delicious!
- In Spain, a **tortilla** *(tohr-tee-yah)* is a potato, onion, and egg omelet that's often served at room temperature.
- In Mexico, **elote** *(eh-loh-teh)* is the name of tender corn, the kind you eat from the cob. The same thing in Argentina, Chile, Peru, and Bolivia is called **choclo** *(choh-kloh).*
- Green beans in Mexico are called **ejotes** *(eh-Hoh-tehs).* In South America, you find them under names like **porotos verdes** *(poh-roh-tohs bvehr-dehs),* or **porotitos** *(poh-roh-tee-tohs).* When the beans are dry, they're called **porotos** *(poh-roh-tohs)* in most of Spanish-speaking America, except in Mexico, where they are known as **frijoles** *(free-Hoh-lehs).* Nowhere else can you see as great a variety of beans as in a Peruvian market. They come in enough colors and shapes and sizes to make your mouth water. You may want to try them all.
- In Chile, **filete** *(fee-leh-teh)* is the cut of beef called "sirloin" in the United States. In Argentina, the same cut is called **lomo** *(loh-moh).*

- The basic Argentinean meal is **bife, con papas y ensalada** *(bvee-feh kohn pah-pahs ee ehn-sah-lah-dah),* which translates to "grilled steak, with potatoes and salad." On an Argentinean grill, you're likely to find a number of meats familiar to you, along with others that you've probably never eaten. Among the more exotic are **chinchulín** *(cheen-choo-leen),* which is braided and grilled beef bowels. **¡Delicioso!** Another delicacy is **molleja** *(moh-lyeh-Hah),* which is the thyroid gland of a cow.
- In Mexico, **molleja** *(moh-yeh-Hah)* is chicken gizzard. And in Chile, the same chicken gizzard is **contre** *(kohn-treh).*
- The liver that you eat in Chile is called **pana** *(pah-nah);* in most other places in Latin America, liver is **hígado** *(ee-gah-doh).*
- In Spain, **jamón serrano** *(Ha-mohn seh-rran-oh),* salt-cured ham typical of the mountain regions, is a great delicacy.

Some people say that what's truly special about Latin American foods is the sauces. This statement is especially true of the sauces served in Mexico, which have an infinite variety of flavors and textures.

Mole *(moh-leh),* a word used in Mexico, means "sauce." These Mexican moles are served hot with meats and chicken:

- **Mole negro** *(moh-leh neh-groh)* (black mole) looks black — naturally! — and is made with all toasted ingredients: cocoa, chilies, almonds, onions, garlic, and bread. It can be very spicy or less so.

- **Mole colorado** *(moh-leh koh-loh-rah-doh)* (red mole) looks red and is made with chilies. It is spicy hot! The sauce is also called **coloradito.**
- **Mole amarillo** *(moh-leh ah-mah-ree-lyoh)* (yellow mole) is orangey yellow. You make it with almonds and raisins, among other ingredients. Generally, it is only mildly spicy.
- **Mole verde** *(moh-leh bvehr-deh)* (green mole) is made with green tomatoes, green chilies (hot peppers), and coriander (cilantro) and looks green. It can be very spicy or mildly hot.

Mexicans don't eat moles every day. These delicacies are served only on special occasions. Tourists are luckier — they can find them all the time.

Mexicans also bring some cold sauces to the table to add more spice to your food.

- **Pico de gallo** *(pee-koh deh gah-lyoh),* which translates as "rooster's beak," is made totally with vegetables. It looks red, green, and white, because it's made with tomatoes, jalapeño peppers, coriander, and onions. Hot!
- **Guacamole** *(gooah-kah-moh-leh)* needs no translation. It's the dip made with avocado, **chili** *(chee-leh)* (hot pepper), coriander (cilantro), lemon, and salt. It's sometimes spicy hot.
- **Salsa verde** (sahl-sah bvehr-deh) is a green sauce made with green tomatoes, chilies, and coriander. Hot!
- **Salsa roja** *(sahl-sah roh-Hah)* is a red sauce is made with red tomatoes and chilies. Hot!

At the Market

In this section, you visit markets that may be open or under a roof but are more informal than supermarkets. Also, in these markets, vendors are salespeople, not just cashiers, and they may approach you to sell you goods that you may or may not want. When you don't want something you can simply say one of the following:

- **Ahora no, gracias.** *(ah-oh-rah noh grah-seeahs)* (Not now, thank you.)
- **Ya tengo, gracias.** *(yah tehn-goh grah-seeahs)* (I already have some, thanks.)
- **No me interesa, gracias.** *(no meh een-teh-reh-sah grah-seeahs)* (It doesn't interest me, thank you.)
- **Más tarde, gracias.** *(mahs tahr-deh grah-seeahs)* (Later, thank you.)
- **No me gusta, gracias.** *(noh meh goos-tah grah-seeahs)* (I don't like it, thanks.)
- **No me moleste, ¡por favor!** *(noh meh moh-lehs-teh pohr fah-bvohr)* (Don't bother me, please!)

You may love markets where you're surrounded by vendors and other people, and enjoy an environment so different from what you're used to. Depending where you go, these markets may be full of folks wearing clothes that you probably haven't seen before, talking and behaving in ways that are new to you.

In most markets in Latin America, merchandise is piled in colorful mountains. You may choose from these items at your leisure.

In supermarkets, prices are clearly posted. In other markets, they're probably not, although this practice varies from country to country. In some places, where prices are not marked, you may be able to negotiate a price by simply protesting that it's too high. The vendors are interested in selling, so they allow some discount.

When you go to the market, it's a good idea to bring your own shopping bags or baskets to carry away the stuff you buy. Supermarkets provide bags, of course, but at the more informal markets, the vendor simply packs the stuff you buy but doesn't provide a larger container to carry it away. Wherever this is the rule, you can find stalls that sell bags or baskets of all sizes. More often than not, you want to take these bags home with you — many of them are handmade and quite beautiful.

Buying fruit

Here are the names of fruits you find at the market:

- **la cereza** *(lah seh-reh-sah)* (the cherry)
- **la ciruela** *(lah see-ro-eh-lah)* (the plum)
- **el durazno** *(ehl doo-rahs-noh)* (the peach); **el melocotón** *(ehl meh-loh-koh-tohn)* [in Spain]
- **la fresa** *(la freh-sah)* (the strawberry) [in Mexico, Central America, and Spain]; **la frutilla** *(lah froo-tee-yah)* (the strawberry) [from Colombia to the South Pole]
- **la guayaba** *(lah gooah-yah-bvah)* (the guava)
- **el higo** *(ehl ee-goh)* (the fig)

- **la lima** *(lah lee-mah)* (lime)
- **el limón** *(ehl lee-mohn)* (the lemon)
- **el mango** *(ehl mahn-goh)* (the mango)
- **la manzana** *(lah mahn-sah-nah)* (the apple)
- **el melón** *(ehl meh-lohn)* (the melon)
- **la mora** *(lah moh-rah)* (the blackberry)
- **la naranja** *(lah nah-rahn-Hah)* (the orange)
- **la papaya** *(lah pah-pah-yah)* (the papaya)
- **la pera** *(lah peh-rah)* (the pear)
- **el plátano** *(ehl plah-tah-noh)* (the banana)
- **el pomelo** *(ehl poh-meh-loh)* (the grapefruit) [in Mexico]; **la toronja** *(lah toh-rohn-Ha)* (the grapefruit) [in other Latin American countries]
- **la sandía** *(lah sahn-deeah)* (the watermelon)
- **la tuna** *(lah too-nah)* (the prickly pear)
- **la uva** *(lah oo-bvah)* (the grape)

Buying vegetables

Fresh vegetables are always good. You can easily find the following:

- **las acelgas** *(lahs ah-sehl-gahs)* (the Swiss chard)
- **el aguacate** *(ehl ah-gooah-kah-teh)* (the avocado); **la palta** *(lah pahl-tah)* (the avocado) [in South America]
- **el ají** *(el ah-Hee)* (the hot pepper) [in South America]; **el chile** *(chee-leh)* (the hot pepper) [in Mexico and Guatemala]

- **el ajo** *(ehl ah-Hoh)* (the garlic)
- **el brócoli** *(ehl bvroh-koh-lee)* (the broccoli)
- **la calabacita** *(lah kah-lah-bvah-see-tah)* (the zucchini) [in Mexico]; **el zapallito** *(ehl sah-pah-yee-toh)* (the zucchini) [in Uruguay and Argentina]
- **la calabaza** *(lah kah-lah-bvah-sah)* (the pumpkin) [in Central America and Mexico]; **el zapallo** *(ehl sah-pah-yoh)* (the pumpkin) [in South America]
- **las cebollas** *(lahs seh-bvoh-yahs)* (the onions)
- **el chile morrón** *(ehl chee-leh moh-rrohn)* (the sweet pepper) [in Mexico]; **el pimentón** *(ehl pee-mehn-tohn)* (the sweet pepper) [in Argentina, Chile, and Uruguay]
- **la col** *(lah kohl)* (the cabbage) [in Mexico]; **el repollo** *(ehl reh-poh-yoh)* (the cabbage) [in Argentina and Chile]
- **la coliflor** *(lah koh-lee-flohr)* (the cauliflower)
- **la espinaca** *(lah ehs-pee-nah-kah)* (the spinach)
- **la lechuga** *(lah leh-choo-gah)* (the lettuce)
- **las papas** *(lahs pah-pahs)* (the potatoes); **patatas** *(pah-tah-tahs)* [in Spain]
- **la zanahoria** *(lah sah-nah-oh-reeah)* (the carrot)

Shopping for fish

These terms can help you when you're selecting fish:

- **el camarón** *(kah-mah-rohn)* (shrimp); **gambas** *(gahm-bahs)* [in Spain]
- **el congrio** *(ehl kohn-greeoh)* (conger eel) [coasts of Chile and Peru]

- **el huachinango** *(ehl ooah-chee-nahn-goh)* (red snapper)
- **el langostino** *(ehl lahn-gohs-tee-noh)* (prawn)
- **el marisco** *(ehl mah-rees-koh)* (seafood)
- **el pescado** *(ehl pehs-kah-doh)* (fish)
- **la trucha** *(lah troo-chah)* (trout)

At the Supermercado

Of course, you can also buy groceries at the **supermercado** *(soo-pehr-mehr-kah-doh),* where you proceed very much as you do in the United States. You may also find food there that you are more accustomed to. The supermarket is a good place to go for things like cereals and canned goods.

Following are some words and phrases that can help you at the supermarket:

- **el arroz** *(ehl ah-rrohs)* (the rice)
- **el atún** *(ehl ah-toon)* (the tuna)
- **el fideo** *(ehl fee-deh-oh)* (the pasta)
- **los cereales** *(lohs seh-reh-ah-lehs)* (the cereals)
- **las galletas** *(lahs gah-yeh-tahs)* (the cookies or crackers)
- **la leche** *(lah leh-cheh)* (the milk)
- **pagar** *(pah-gahr)* (to pay)
- **el pasillo** *(ehl pah-see-yoh)* (the aisle)

- **las sardinas** *(lahs sahr-dee-nahs)* (the sardines)
- **el vino** *(ehl bvee-noh)* (the wine)
- **el vuelto** *(ehl bvooehl-toh)* (change [as in money back]); **la vuelta** *(lah bvoo-ehl-tah)* [in Spain]
- **las ollas** *(lahs oh-yas)* (pots)
- **el tercer pasillo** *(ehl tehr-sehr pah-see-yoh)* (the third aisle)
- **al fondo** *(ahl fohn-doh)* (at the back)
- **Gracias, aquí está su vuelto.** *(grah-seeahs ah-kee ehs-tah soo bvooehl-toh)* (Thanks, here's your change.)

Dummies Books — Plain-English Solutions for Everyday Challenges

Home & Business Computer Basics

Excel 2007 All-in-One Desk Reference For Dummies	9780470037386	$29.99/$35.99 CAN
MacBook For Dummies	9780470048597	$21.99/$25.99 CAN
Office 2007 All-in-One Desk Reference For Dummies	9780471782797	$29.99/$35.99 CAN
PCs All-in-One Desk Reference For Dummies, 4th Edition	9780470223383	$29.99/$35.99 CAN
PCs For Dummies, 11th Edition	9780470137284	$21.99/$25.99 CAN
Troubleshooting Your PC For Dummies	9780764516696	$24.99/$37.99 CAN
Upgrading & Fixing PCs For Dummies	9780764516658	$21.99/$32.99 CAN
Windows XP All-in-One Desk Reference For Dummies	9780471749417	$29.99/$35.99 CAN
Windows Vista For Dummies	9780471754213	$21.99/$25.99 CAN
Windows Vista For Dummies, Quick Reference	9780471783268	$16.99/$19.99 CAN
Word 2007 For Dummies	9780470036587	$21.99/$25.99 CAN
CD & DVD Recording For Dummies	9780764516276	$21.99/$32.99 CAN

Internet & Digital Media

Digital Photography All-in-One Desk Reference For Dummies, 3rd Edition	9780470037430	$35.99/$47.99 CAN
Geneology For Dummies	9780764508073	$24.99/$37.99 CAN
Internet All-in-One Desk Reference For Dummies	9780764516597	$29.99/$44.99 CAN
Internet For Dummies, 11th Edition	9780470121740	$21.99/$25.99 CAN
Search Engine Optimization For Dummies, 2nd Edition	9780471979982	$24.99/$29.99 CAN
iPhone For Dummies	9780470174692	$21.99/$25.99 CAN
AppleTV For Dummies	9780470173626	$21.99/$25.99 CAN
Photoshop Elements 2 For Dummies	9780764516757	$21.99/$32.99 CAN
YouTube For Dummies	9780470149256	$21.99/$25.99 CAN

Graphics & Web Development

Flash CS3 For Dummies	9780470121009	$24.99/$29.99 CAN
ASP.NET For Dummies	9780764508660	$24.99/$37.99 CAN
Dreamweaver CS3 For Dummies	9780470114902	$24.99/$29.99 CAN
iMac For Dummies, 4th Edition	9780764584589	$21.99/$25.99 CAN
InDesign CS3 For Dummies	9780470118658	$24.99/$29.99 CAN
Macs For Dummies, 9th Edition	9780470048498	$21.99/$25.99 CAN
Photoshop CS3 All-in-One Desk Reference For Dummies	9780470111956	$39.99/$47.99 CAN
Photoshop CS3 For Dummies	9780470111932	$24.99/$29.99 CAN
PowerPoint 2007 For Dummies	9780470040591	$21.99/$25.99 CAN
Web Design For Dummies, 2nd Edition	9780471781172	$24.99/$31.99 CAN